THE
SECRET
THAT LIES
BENEATH

Richard A. Morris

STRATTON
—PRESS—
Publishing Life

The Secret that Lies Beneath
Copyright © 2020 **Richard A. Morris**

Stratton Press Publishing
831 N Tatnall Street Suite M #188,
Wilmington, DE 19801
www.stratton-press.com
1-888-323-7009

ISBN (Paperback): 978-1-64345-308-8
ISBN (Ebook): 978-1-64895-112-1

Printed in the United States of America

Throughout *The Secret That Lies Beneath*, it is apparent that love can appear in many different forms. Being in love is one of the greatest emotions that can be shared between two individuals. One should learn to take their time to truly understand their partners and how they behave during different roles in which they are forced to play.

One should trust slowly, and each day will bring to you opportunities and challenges that allow you to learn about yourself and your partner. Finding love with another individual is a gift. Through communication, individuals in love will continue to experience and build upon their intimacy. Although expressing one's thoughts and feelings may make one feel vulnerable, the gain in intimacy and increased love is exponential. However, it is very important to realize during the period of building a healthy and nurturing relationship, it does not warrant that you should jeopardize your mental and physical health. Take care of your body and mind for they are your gift to another person.

Wishing you all peace, good health, and love!

I dedicate this book to all the innocent, loving, caring men and women who have opened their hearts and souls, believing what has so readily sprung forth from the deceitful secret whose identity will shortly be revealed that lies beneath the zipper. I hope that reading this book will help you heal your injuries and wounds. May you find peace and your soul find happiness from within. May you be strong!

This book would not be possible without my dear friend, Mary Ann. Although we are new in each other's lives, we now believe we will find the right man.

It is through our laughter, crying, hugging, appreciation, and support for one another that this book is possible.

PREFACE

It seems that life is about timing. From the moment we take our first breath when we are born and throughout the rest of our lives, we can attribute timing to the good or challenging situations that we encounter.

We question timing every moment of the day when we think to ourselves, "Hurry, make the yellow light so we are not late picking up the kids from soccer practice" or "Why did I lose my job?" or "Why did the relationship have to end?"

Did you ever wonder that there is perhaps a reason that the traffic light turned a particular color and there is a reason for the ending of a relationship?

I have no regrets in life. This belief helps me cope with the challenging situations that I am faced with every day. It leads me to believe that any negative event or occurrence that I encounter will result in a lesson for me. In turn, I am able to share my story with someone else so that they are able to process data and cope better with their situations.

Maybe there is a greater power that we are not aware of that causes us to encounter the red light or the ending to a perfect relationship. Perhaps we will never know the answer. Being born at one second later could result in new pathways of lessons, experiences, and different people that are brought into our lives.

Timing Is Everything: New Career

I had always wanted to move to New York City from Boston because Boston no longer offered to me the opportunities to meet new people and my days were so predictable. I was in a rut and wondering what am I going to do with my life. The timing for the job offer was perfect. It would allow me so many new challenges with a job and new people to meet.

Timing Is Everything: New Relationship

One of the greatest lessons that I learned about relationships occurred at a Halloween party several months after I moved to NYC. A man walked into the room who I had never met. His presence took my breath away. I felt an attraction to him like no other individual. Both of us felt this energy and decided it was worth to explore dating. However, in about seven months, this man went from being my soul mate to being a detriment to my mental health. I allowed him to begin to change my essence and soul because I tried to change to make him love me the way I wanted to be loved.

After two years of being in a bad situation, I ended it. I needed to regain back my confidence and take care of myself. This newfound confidence resulted in me giving off a more positive energy.

Timing Is Everything: Relocate to Miami Beach, Florida

The hotel company that I was working for in NYC offered me a position in their two hotels in Miami Beach. I welcomed the change of a new job. It was during this change to a new city that I realized the power that I allowed someone to have over me. It was during this time that I thought about writing a self-help book about the healing of broken hearts.

It took me about three years to collect my ideas. After this period, it allowed me to present my ideas and vision for this self-help book to a graphic artist, who put my dream onto paper. In April 2014, my dream, *The Secret That Lies Beneath*, was published.

There are many reasons that I wrote *The Secret That Lies Beneath*. Some of the reasons are:

- For individuals to realize that the purpose of dating is to collect data. To use this acquired information to help us make informed decisions about our potential partner.
- For there to be one less broken heart in the world.
- To have one less individual lay in their bed unable to move, eat, or sleep because of their broken heart.
- For a person to never doubt what they had done wrong as to the reasons why Percy Pecker had left them.
- For a person to take away valuable lessons from the ending of their relationship.
- For a person to learn that they are a gift for someone else. If someone does not appreciate them for their qualities, then they are not the right individual for you.

I hope that the reader will never give up their search for their Prince Percy.

Timing Is Everything: Republish and Redesign My Book

About fourteen months after my book was published, I was approached with the opportunity to change the style and branding of my book, *The Secret That Lies Beneath*. After surveying many bookstores around the country, their feedback helped me realize that if I wanted to reach the right demographic and have the purpose of my book understood by the right audience, I needed to make some significant changes.

I embraced this the feedback because it gave me another opportunity to change the style and wording of my book. If we allow changes and new challenges in life, it helps us define who we are today. I get upset with the statements "if only I knew this beforehand" or "what if." It was the perfect timing for me to redesign my book because over the years, I have developed an audience of readers around the world that will help me share the news of my newly designed book.

In summary, change is good. Change brings us lessons and knowledge to use for the future. Lessons bring us greatness. It causes change, growth, and confidence in us that allows us to continue to redesign ourselves and attract new people in our life.

I hope that each reader will gain some insight to who they are as a person. The book will cause readers to look into their hearts and souls from the words on the pages that I put so much time and energy to write *The Secret That Lies Beneath*.

The Quiet Abstractions…questions in my restless mind about the "Secret."

It is the most well-kept secret in the world.

One does not need a license or permit to carry and use it.

The Secret, also referred to as a weapon, does not go off at airport security checkpoints.

It is often used by individuals unaware of its potential impact and damage.

The time has come to disclose this hidden, dangerous secret used by all men: black and white, straight and gay.

It is genetically referred to as the penis, but throughout this short story, better known as Percy Pecker, a sophisticated and debonair character.

...genetically referred to as the Penis.
But throughout this short story,
better known as

PERCY PECKER

The Secret that Lies Beneath

This story, although short, has finally given me the answers that I feel have constantly haunted most men and women. Percy Pecker leaves behind so many questions regarding the ending of a relationship. Unfortunately, we never get the closure on these questions that would allow us to move forward in life.

The worst result occurs when we are left in a state of limbo.

Percy Pecker, usually concealed or locked behind bars (jean zippers), has caused us to:

- seek therapy for broken hearts
- suffer from insomnia
- overeat and undereat
- self-medicate with mood stabilizers, tranquilizers, and sleeping pills
- pursue emotionally unavailable and unpredictable Percys
- take our own lives

Percy is capable of bringing tears to our eyes, spasms to our body that is caused by the incredible pleasure and joy he brings us.

Ironically, Percy can feel like a knife through our heart and to bring us such uncontrollable pain that we ultimately feel as though we have chest pains so painful that we need to call 911?

Why do we allow Percy to enter into our hearts and souls?

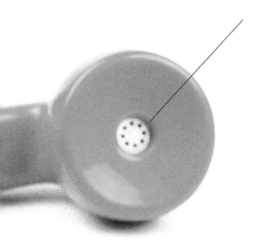

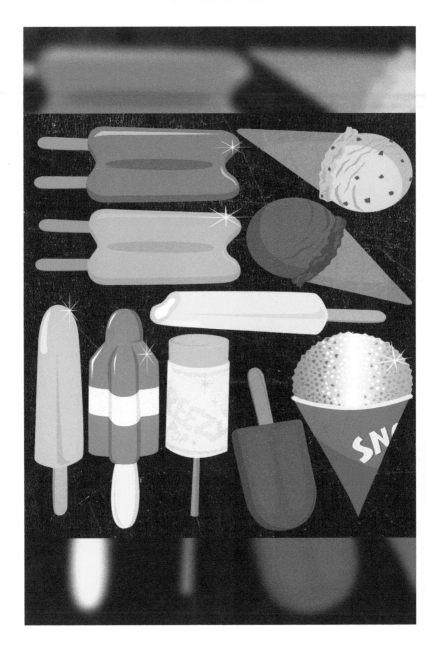

Getting Schooled by Percy

High School
The Age of Innocence
This is the highest chance to have your heart broken but you are
not aware yet of what is actually happening Entry-level lines
often used by Percy: "You are my first" and "The back seat of my
car is really comfortable"

College
The First Stage of Adulthood
The first semester begins with one-night stands You begin to
realize there is a pattern to the lines and resulting actions from
Percy You now compare them to the lines you hear from your
friends You now realize that Percy has its own language "My
roommate knows this is a special night and has left us alone Let
me finish lighting the candles and opening this bottle of wine" The
opening of the wine is the last "pop" you'll hear from your beloved
Percy on your romantic night Your heart will now be broken and
you'll ask your friends for the name of a good therapist

Master's Degree
All Defenses Up
All defenses are set for go However Percy has seen this level of
education and all defense mechanisms are operating This
actually stimulates the challenge of Percy Pecker He will be
victorious You will be the loser and ask your therapist for
antidepressants because you can no longer function day to day

The Lesson of Life and Percy Pecker
The more money we invest in our education the more that we
think we know about the Standard Operating Procedure of Percy
Pecker This is actually an oxymoron: the more education we have
the less we know about the inner workings of the Lethal Weapon

This list is intended to be exhaustive in descending order o importance in each section:

Sexual
1. erotic pleasure, especially via the ridged band and Meissner corpuscles
2. acts as a rolling bearing in intercourse and masturbation
3. prevents dyspareunia (painful intercourse)
4. stimulates partner's genitalia, giving erotic pleasure
5. supplies skin to cover the shaft in erection and prevent tightness
6. stores pheromones and releases them on arousal
7. stores and releases natural lubricants ("smegma" and pre-ejaculator fluid)
8. makes the glans a visual signal of sexual arousal
9. provides a seal against the vaginal wall to contain semen

Protective
1. prevents the glans becoming keratinized and keeps it soft and mois
2. protects the thin-skinned glans against injury
3. protects the nerves of the glans, retaining their erotic function
4. in infancy, protects the urethra against contamination, meatal ste nosis, and UTIs
5. provides lysosomes for bacteriostatic action around the glans
6. pigmented, it protects the unpigmented glans against sunburn
7. vascular (rich in blood vessels that bring heat to the tissues), i protects the less vascular glans against frostbite, as Sir Randolp Fiennes found on his epic transpolar walk

Other
1. provides skin for grafts to burnt eyelids, reconstructive surgery, etc
2. storage of contact lenses, smuggled jewels, etc.

THE QUESTIONS THAT
HAUNT OUR MIND

Answers to be revealed throughout this book:

1. How can something so small cause so much damage?
2. Why didn't Percy call?
3. Why do I smell someone else's perfume/cologne on Percy's clothes?
4. What is the receipt of the Four Star Hotel doing in Percy's briefcase?
5. Why is the lube almost gone?
6. I thought the box of condoms was full.
7. Percy told me he got rid of his screen names on sex sites.
8. Percy's manager called me asking if I enjoyed the play last night with the tickets that he gave him to surprise me. I never saw a play last night. Percy said he worked on a project all night.
9. Percy said he couldn't have sex with me because he was too tired from work. His manager called me

from work today asking if his flu had gotten better and if he was returning to work tomorrow.

10. Why does Percy spend so much time at the gym with his trainer, yet he wasn't losing more weight or getting more buff?

11. Percy told me his "heart" hadn't felt this way in years. So why hasn't he called me a week after our first night of intimacy?

12. Percy told me he would be back in fifteen minutes. He was just going for coffee. That was a week ago.

13. Percy said he was going to introduce me to his parents. I keep looking for them on the side of the milk carton.

14. Percy said he wanted to travel with me, but he has not purchased any tickets.

15. Percy said he would spend quality time with me bike riding, but the bikes continue to get rusty.

16. Percy told me that I could start bringing clothes to his house. So why did we break up the next morning?

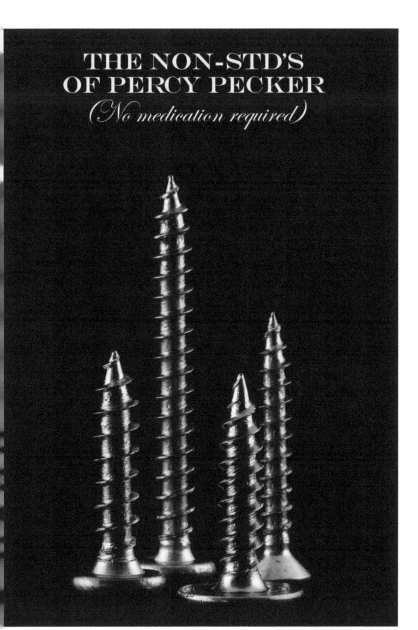

THE NON-STD'S
OF PERCY PECKER
(No medication required)

CONFRONTATION AND RESPONSE OF PERCY

Communication
Text messaging
E-mail
Voice mail

Commitment
"Honestly, can we talk about it tomorrow? I'm tired."

No rules or explanations required when ending a relationship. Ultimately, leaves their partner questions that never receive answers.

Intimacy
Text messaging
E-mail
Voice mail
Watching TV during a conversation of importance
"I am about to take a shower, let's talk about this in the morning."

Thinking of sports or a porno movie during your wedding/commitment ceremony

Monogamy
What is that?
Impossible…
The "Don't ask, don't tell" rule applies
What they don't know won't hurt them It's only sex.
I can separate sex from feelings…nothing to worry about

A Chained Soul
Rarely saying "I love you"

Richard A. Morris

Stories with no endings

Why did Percy leave me?

Maybe if I had done "this or that" he wouldn't have left me?

Maybe if I buy him flowers?

Maybe if I make him a romantic dinner?

Maybe I can change to make him love me?

How many times have these thoughts gone through our minds?

How many times in a day?

How many times during conversations with friends and family?

How many times during meetings at work?

How many of us have gone to therapy to try and figure out what is wrong with *us*?

Richard A. Morris

the
Conspiracy
Theory

Why has nothing been done to reveal the Secret?
Why is there no schooling to teach men the rights
and wrongs of Percy?
Why are there no laws to license the use of Percy?
Why haven't the leaders of the world taken action
against the potential damage Percy can cause to the
hearts and minds of innocent men and women?

Name _____

Address _____ Date _____

R~X~

MD _____ *the Secret?*

Signature _____

t only stands to reason that there
are others in on the secret…

Could it be a conspiracy of the
American Psychiatric Association
and the Food and Drug
Administration?

What would all the licensed psy-
chologists and psychiatrists do
with their extra time?

Who would consume all the
Prozac, Lexapro, Xanax, Klonopin,
and Valium?

The stocks of pharmaceutical compa-
nies would plummet. Researchers of
new drugs would be out of jobs.

f Percy Pecker is running rampant
with no restrictions or accountability,
then there will be continued endless
questions, resulting in countless broken hearts and emergency visits to
psychiatrists and emergency wards and
drugstores.

This translates to rising pharmaceutical stock prices and stockholder
profits. Perhaps it is greed for
money that allows Percy to run rampant throughout the cities and countries
of the world.

We have learned through our experiences that Percy appears many different disguises and roles. He is a chameleon that is successful in obtaining his needs from us. He defines success through the achievement, attainment, breakthrough, fortune, happiness, reward, triumph, and victory over others. He has graduated summa cum laude from the most expensive theatrical university in the world and has proved his talent. Through his years of education, he has mastered the role and appearance of many:

A sophisticated and debonair character that we want to introduce to our families, a butch man, religious figure, athlete, flight attendant, restaurant manager, top-selling salesman, attorney, doctor, artist, political official, therapist, and author. Remember that although Percy may take any form, the heart will not discriminate against him. Neither will it discriminate in terms of age, wealth, status in society, race, color, size, shape, or religion.

Our Prince Percy is out there: a genuine, caring, communicative, sincere, and loving human being. We will find him when we have learned and embraced our past. You are an incredible person that only few will be fortunate to love. Trust is earned so open your heart slowly. You are in possession to give the most valuable treasure you can offer another: your soul, commitment, and heart.

MORE ANSWERS

The greatest, most valuable lesson I have learned is that we won't necessarily find the answer to every action of Percy. That's okay. We hate limbo.

For every action, there must be an answer. The best lesson I have learned resulted from the biggest burden lifted from my heart: I have learned that it is okay not to have the answer.

So stop the crying, stop the medication, stop the therapy...just get off the couch. The answer is already within you.

Embrace the new you!

The greatest lesson that I have learned occurred while writing this book. There were so many questions that haunted my mind and soul for all the reasons that Percy treated me the way that he did when I didn't deserve his actions.

It is now years later, as I finish the last chapters of this book, that I realize that I never got the answers to all those questions from years ago. Coming to this epiphany was an incredible weight being lifted from my heart and soul. I felt like a new person taking their first breath in life again!

After reaching this conclusion and answers to all my questions, I offered the following advice to those suffering from broken hearts: "Stop the crying, get off the sofa, stop the therapy and medication, there is nothing wrong with you." You are a great person and you need to embrace who you are as a person.

Realize that you are a gift for another individual, and together, we will make all of our dreams come true.

THE CONCLUSION

Inner strength and endurance against the concealed weapon of Percy Pecker.

We should never look back on our relationships. Each experience, bad or good, has brought us to where we are today. It is a place of lessons learned and a place of higher being. We should value our lessons and embrace them, for they have brought people and journeys into our lives. These experiences will bring us strength, independence, and acceptance even in defeat.

With every goodbye, we learn that it will bring us to a better state of being and happiness. For the most exciting relationship of all is the one you have with yourself.

CPSIA information can be obtained
at www.ICGtesting.com
Printed in the USA
LVHW071625200820
663741LV00021B/2074